Write the missing uppercase or lowercase letter for each letter of the alphabet.

A a B b   c D

E F   g h

I j K l

m N o P

   t

q

U V w X

Y z

Circle the two pictures in each row that begin with the same sound.

CD-104353

© Carson-Dellosa

at

og

ar

ite

ope

ish

eaf

est

oat

Circle the two pictures in each row that end with the same sound.

CD-104353

© Carson-Dellosa

Say the name of each picture. Write the letter of the ending sound to complete the name.

pe___

ba___

bu___

fro___

sta___

sle___

soa___

boo___

dru___

© Carson-Dellosa

CD-104353

Circle the two pictures in each row with names that rhyme.

CD-104353 © Carson-Dellosa

Write the beginning letter of each word to complete the word.

at

at

at

en

en

en

op

op

op

ug

ug

ug

© Carson-Dellosa

CD-104353

Say the name of each picture. Fill in the circle beside the correct name.

○ map
○ mop
○ man

○ bun
○ sand
○ sun

○ car
○ cow
○ can

○ bell
○ wall
○ ball

○ book
○ hook
○ back

○ rake
○ cake
○ cape

○ clock
○ clown
○ coat

○ sat
○ stop
○ star

○ horse
○ horn
○ house

CD-104353

© Carson-Dellosa

Circle the word that names each picture.

sock socks	frog frogs	apple apples
boat boats	fly flies	box boxes
baby babies	bus buses	foot feet
glass glasses	mouse mice	leaf leaves

© Carson-Dellosa   CD-104353   **9**

Say the name of each picture. Write the letter of the short vowel sound to complete the name.

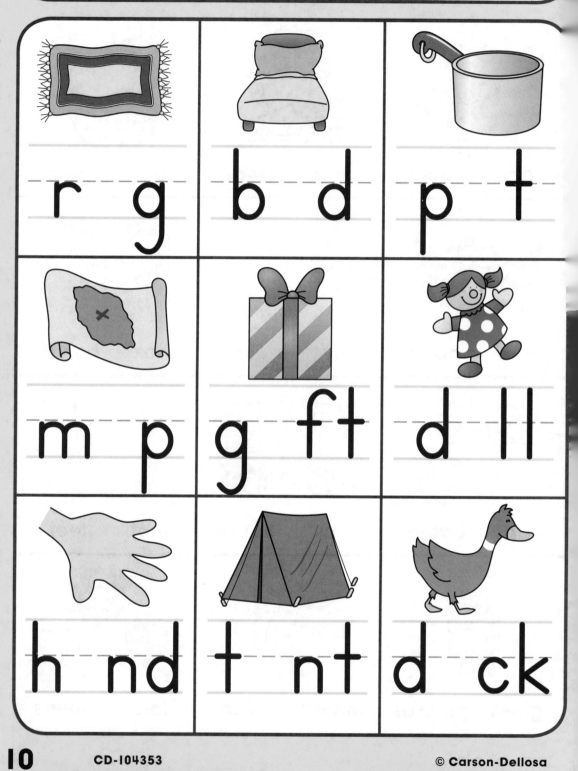

r g   b d   p t

m p   g ft   d ll

h nd   t nt   d ck

 CD-104353   © Carson-Dellosa

Say the name of each picture. Circle the words in each row that have the long vowel sound shown.

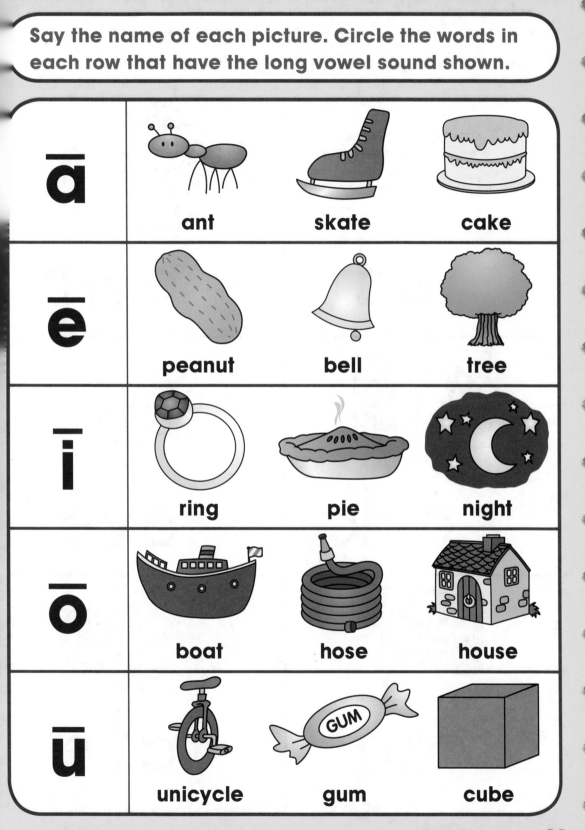

ā	ant	skate	cake
ē	peanut	bell	tree
ī	ring	pie	night
ō	boat	hose	house
ū	unicycle	gum	cube

© Carson-Dellosa   CD-104353

Say the name of each picture. Write the letters of the beginning blend to complete the name.

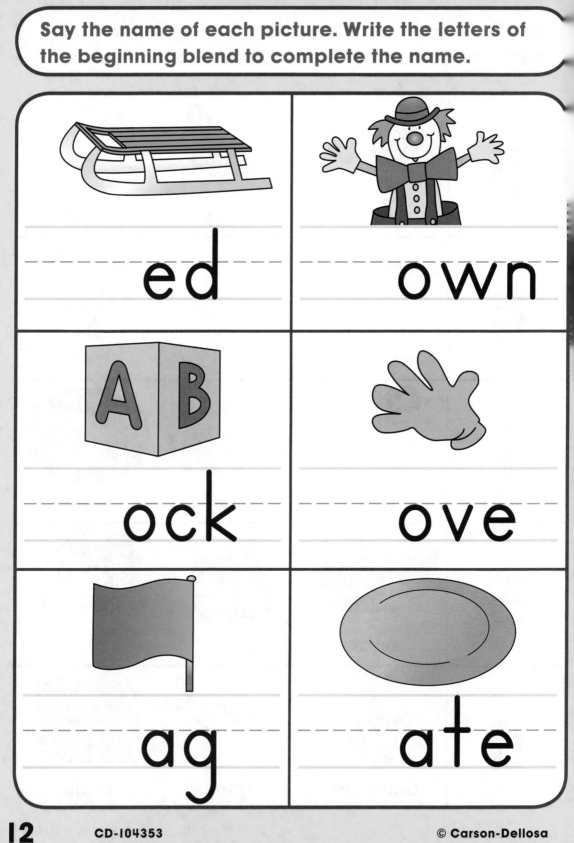

ed

own

ock

ove

ag

ate

CD-104353   © Carson-Dellosa

Say the name of each picture. Write the letters of the beginning blend to complete the name.

um

ush

own

ain

og

apes

sh

th

ch

qu

wh

CD-104353

© Carson-Dellosa

Circle the correct word to complete each sentence.

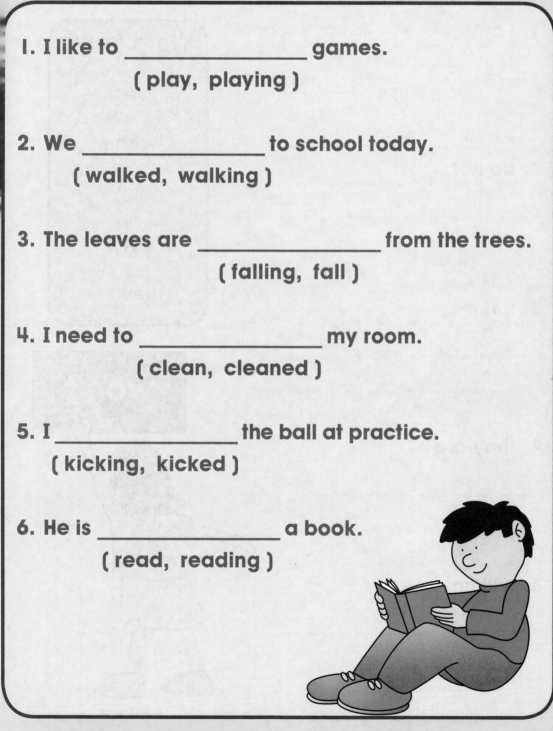

1. I like to _____ games.
   (play, playing)

2. We _____ to school today.
   (walked, walking)

3. The leaves are _____ from the trees.
   (falling, fall)

4. I need to _____ my room.
   (clean, cleaned)

5. I _____ the ball at practice.
   (kicking, kicked)

6. He is _____ a book.
   (read, reading)

Write the correct contraction for each pair of words.

1. I am

_____

2. do not

_____

3. it is

_____

4. they are

_____

5. will not

_____

Word Bank

it's

won't

I'm

don't

they're

won't

CD-104353   © Carson-Dellosa

Circle the correct pronoun to complete each sentence.

1. Denise likes sports.

   _____ is good at bowling.

   (It, She)

2. Juan and Dante play basketball.

   _____ are on the same team.

   (They, We)

3. My sister and I are learning to play tennis.

   _____ are beginners.

   (He, We)

4. This is a new baseball bat.

   _____ is made of wood.

   (She, It)

© Carson-Dellosa CD-104353

Draw a line to connect the words that make a compound word.

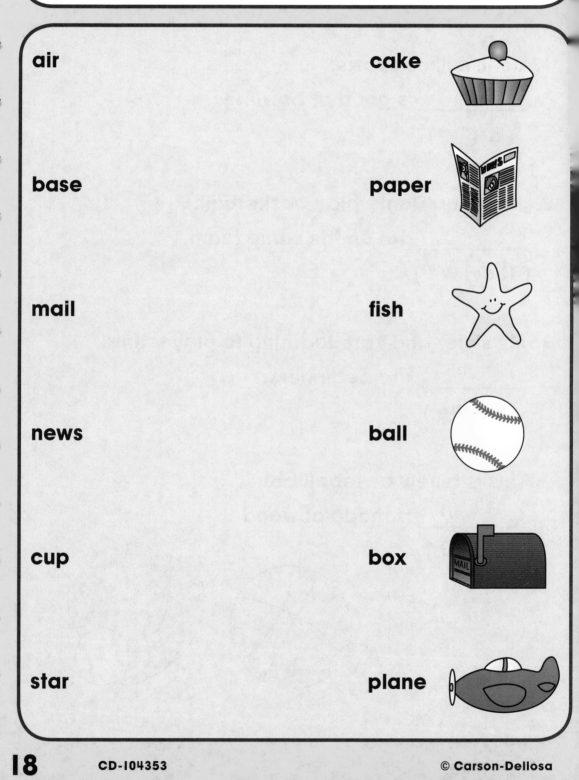

air   cake

base   paper

mail   fish

news   ball

cup   box

star   plane

© Carson-Dellosa

Draw a line from each word to its opposite.

happy   little

big   right

up   slow

left   off

fast   under

hot   sad

on   cold

over   down

© Carson-Dellosa   CD-104353

Draw a line from each word to the word that means the same thing.

begin	pal
correct	grin
happy	right
smile	glad
gift	start
yell	present
alike	shout
friend	same

© Carson-Dellosa

Write the words from the word bank in **ABC** order.

Word Bank

frog

up

man

jump

apple

sun

door

Circle the picture in each row that matches the sentence.

The boy is flying a kite.

The girl is building a snowman.

The cat has black stripes.

The dog has a green collar.

 CD-104353 © Carson-Dellosa

Unscramble each group of words to form a sentence.

1. The   soft.   is   cat

_____

_____

2. the   is   She   rug.   on

_____

_____

3. is   name   Fuzz.   Her

_____

_____

4. wake   Do   not   her.

_____

_____

Circle the correct punctuation mark to complete each sentence.

1. We went sailing   .   ?

2. The wind was strong   .   ?

3. Have you ever been sailing   .   ?

4. Our boat had two sails   .   ?

5. Do you like boats   .   ?

6. We saw many other boats   .   ?

7. I had a good time   .   ?

8. When will we go again   .   ?

CD-104353
© Carson-Dellosa

Number the pictures in the order in which they happened.

Finally, the airplane rolls into the hangar.

First, the airplane flies through the sky.

Next, the airplane lands at the airport.

© Carson-Dellosa

CD-104353

Look at the picture. Then, answer each question.

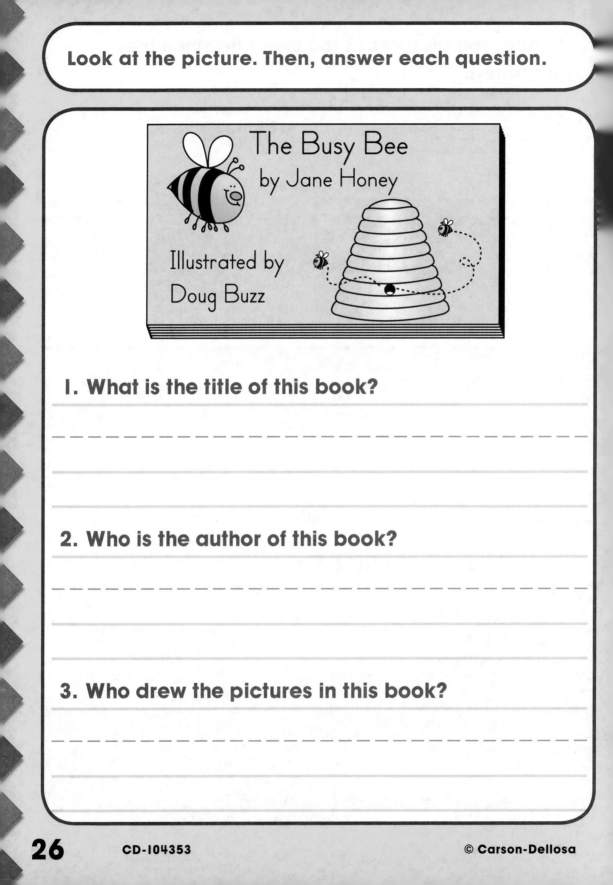

The Busy Bee
by Jane Honey

Illustrated by
Doug Buzz

1. **What is the title of this book?**

_____

_____

2. **Who is the author of this book?**

_____

_____

3. **Who drew the pictures in this book?**

_____

_____

CD-104353

© Carson-Dellosa

Circle the picture if it could really happen. Draw an X on the picture if it could not happen.

1. We go skating.

2. A girl waters flowers.

3. A worm wears glasses.

4. A dog flies a kite.

5. A boy builds a sand castle.

6. The boys play basketball.

7. A man reads the newspaper.

8. A pencil goes for a walk.

© Carson-Dellosa

Read the story. Then, answer each question.

Byron went for a hike in a park. He saw a lot of birds. He jumped over a small rock. Then, he picked up a leaf. Byron had fun.

1. Where did Byron go?

_____

_____

2. What did Byron see?

_____

_____

3. What did Byron pick up?

_____

_____

 CD-104353 © Carson-Dellosa

Draw a line from each event to the event that happened next.

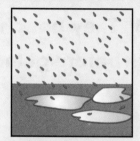

It started to rain.

He read a story.

Phil saw a flower.

Laura built a snowman.

Sean picked out a book.

Rosa used an umbrella.

There was a snow day.

He painted a picture.

1. **José and Derrick went to the mall. They bought new shoes. They ate pizza for lunch before going home.**

   O José and Derrick went to the mall.

   O José and Derrick ate pizza for lunch.

   O José and Derrick bought new shoes.

2. **Leah and Amy played on the swings. They fed the ducks. Leah and Amy had fun at the park.**

   O Leah and Amy played on the swings.

   O Leah and Amy had fun at the park.

   O Leah and Amy fed the ducks.

3. **Uri and Evan went to the beach. They found shells and played in the sand. They also went swimming.**

   O Uri and Evan went swimming.

   O Uri and Evan played in the sand.

   O Uri and Evan went to the beach.

 © Carson-Dellosa

Page 1
The missing letters should be written.
Page 2
The following pictures should be circled: Row 1: moon, mouse; Row 2: bed, bee; Row 3: sun, sock; Row 4: turtle, top; Row 5: hat, house
Page 3
Row 1: cat, dog, jar; Row 2: kite, rope, fish; Row 3: leaf, nest, goat
Page 4
The following pictures should be circled: Row 1: train, spoon; Row 2: net, goat; Row 3: bell, doll; Row 4: web, crab; Row 5: drum, gum
Page 5
Row 1: pen, bat, bus; Row 2: frog, star, sled; Row 3: soap, book, drum
Page 6
The following pictures should be circled: Row 1: bag, flag; Row 2: ring, king; Row 3: bee, key; Row 4: lamp, stamp; Row 5: bear, chair
Page 7
From left to right and top to bottom: Box 1: cat, hat, bat; Box 2: hen, pen, ten; Box 3: top, hop, mop; Box 4: rug, mug, bug
Page 8
Row 1: mop, sun, car; Row 2: ball, book, cake; Row 3: clown, star, horse
Page 9
Row 1: socks, frog, apple; Row 2: boat, flies, box; Row 3: babies, bus, feet; Row 4: glass, mouse, leaves
Page 10
Row 1: rug, bed, pot; Row 2: map, gift, doll; Row 3: hand, tent, duck

Page 11
Row 1: skate, cake; Row 2: peanut, tree; Row 3: pie, night; Row 4: boat, hose; Row 5: unicycle, cube
Page 12
Row 1: sled, clown; Row 2: block, glove; Row 3: flag, plate
Page 13
Row 1: drum, brush; Row 2: crown, train; Row 3: frog, grapes
Page 14

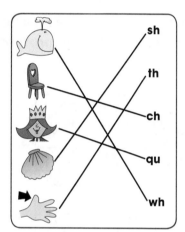

Page 15
1. play; 2. walked; 3. falling; 4. clean; 5. kicked; 6. reading
Page 16
1. I'm; 2. don't; 3. it's; 4. they're; 5. won't
Page 17
1. She; 2. They; 3. We; 4. It
Page 18
Lines should be drawn to make the following words: airplane, baseball, mailbox, newspaper, cupcake, starfish.

Answer Key

Page 19

Lines should be drawn between the following words: happy/sad, big/little, up/down, left/right, fast/slow, hot/cold, on/off, over/under.

Page 20

Lines should be drawn between the following words: begin/start, correct/right, happy/glad, smile/grin, gift/present, yell/shout, alike/same, friend/pal.

Page 21

The words should be in the following order: apple, door, frog, jump, man, sun, up.

Page 22

Page 23

1. The cat is soft.; 2. She is on the rug.; 3. Her name is Fuzz.; 4. Do not wake her.

Page 24

1. .   2. .   3. ?   4. .
5. ?   6. .   7. .   8. ?

Page 25

1. First, the airplane flies through the sky.; 2. Next, the airplane lands at the airport.; 3. Finally, the airplane rolls into the hangar.

Page 26

1. *The Busy Bee*; 2. Jane Honey; 3. Doug Buzz

Page 27

Pictures 1, 2, 5, 6, and 7 should be circled.; Pictures 3, 4, and 8 should have Xs drawn on them.

Page 28

1. Byron went to a park.; 2. Byron saw a lot of birds.; 3. Byron picked up a leaf.

Page 29

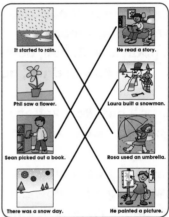

Page 30

1. José and Derrick went to the mall.;
2. Leah and Amy had fun at the park.;
3. Uri and Evan went to the beach.

Page 31

The stars should be colored according to the directions.

Page 32

The shapes should be colored and labeled according to the directions. The total number of triangles is 3.

Page 33

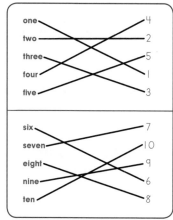

Page 34
The picture should show a cow.

Page 35
The missing numbers should be written.

Page 36
A. 46; B. 60; C. 12; D. 87; E. 93; F. 35;
G. 67; H. 82; I. 45; J. 80; K. 26; L. 99;
M. 6, 8; N. 20, 22; O. 33, 35; P. 58, 60;
Q. 62, 64; R. 71, 73

Page 37
A. 5, 6, 8, 9; B. 20, 25, 35; C. 10, 12, 16;
D. 48, 50, 51; E. 7, 9, 15; F. 30, 50, 60;
G. 12, 15, 24

Page 38
Row 1: circle; Row 2: flower;
Row 3: pumpkin; Row 4: rabbit;
Row 5: apple

Page 39

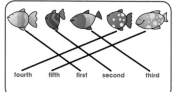

The fish should be colored according
to the directions.

Page 40
A. 34; B. 51; C. 77; D. 13; E. 68; F. 80

Page 41
A. <; B. >; C. <; D. <; E. >; F. >; G. <;
H. >; I. >; J. >; K. <; L. >; M. >; N. <;
O. <; P. >

Page 42
A. 6; B. 9; C. 10; D. 10

Page 43
A. 9; B. 6; C. 9; D. 9; E. 4; F. 9; G. 9;
H. 9; I. 6; Suns A, C, D, F, G, and H
should be colored.

Page 44
A. 7, 8, 4, 6; B. 9, 6, 10, 6; C. 7, 9, 6, 10;
D. 10, 10, 8, 5; E. 5, 8, 3, 7

Page 45
A. 4; B. 4; C. 9; D. 2; E. 4

Page 46
A. 3; B. 3; C. 2; D. 3; E. 2; F. 1;
G. 3; H. 3; I. 3; Stars A, B, D, G, H, and I
should be colored.

Page 47
The picture should show a lighthouse.

Page 48
A. 5, 2, 3, 3; B. 4, 6, 4, 10; C. 4, 7, 3, 4;
D. 3, 1, 3, 1

Page 49
A. 5; B. 9; C. 9; D. 6; E. 7; F. 10; G. 8; H. 9;
I. 6; J. 10; K. 7; L. 10

Page 50
1. Gavin; 2. Juliet; 3. 15;
1. 3; 2. 9; 3. 10; 4. 19

Page 51
A. 40; B. 94; C. 90; D. 59; E. 93;
F. 99; G. 78; H. 67; I. 96; J. 66; K. 27;
L. 48

Page 52
A. 60; B. 56; C. 3; D. 19; E. 10; F. 50;
G. 16; H. 2; I. 53; J. 47; K. 13; L. 10

Answer Key

Page 53

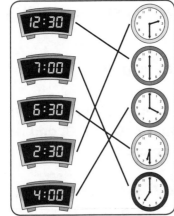

Page 58
1. January: 7, February: 6, November: 1;
2. 22 days

Page 59
The circle, square, and rhombus should be circled.

Page 60
The shapes should be colored according to the directions.

Page 54
B. 1:30; C. 10:00; D. 6:00; E. 9:30; F. 8:00

Page 55
1. Wednesday; 2. 5; 3. Tuesday

Page 56
1. 4; 2. 2; 3. 5; 4. 1; 5. 12

Page 57

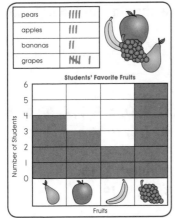

Follow the directions in each row.

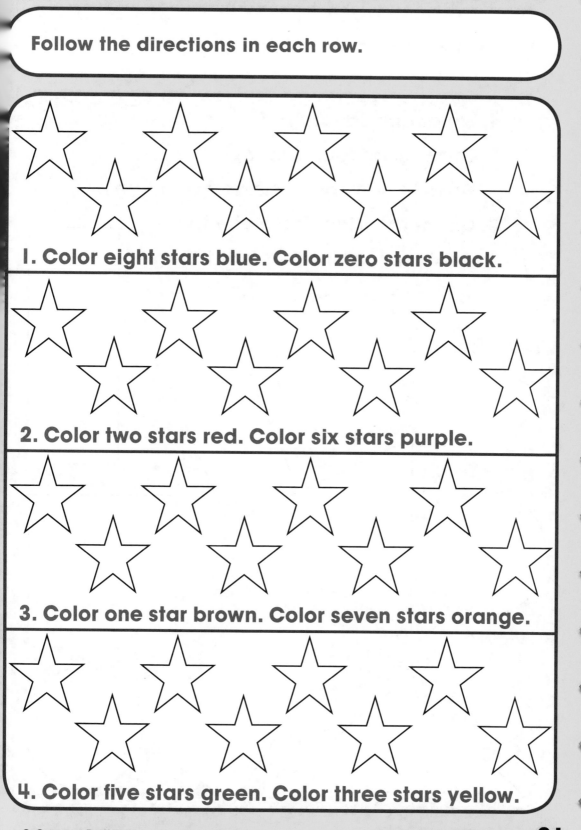

1. Color eight stars blue. Color zero stars black.

2. Color two stars red. Color six stars purple.

3. Color one star brown. Color seven stars orange.

4. Color five stars green. Color three stars yellow.

© Carson-Dellosa CD-104353

1. Color one square red.
2. Draw Xs on four rectangles.
3. Draw smiley faces inside two circles.
4. Count the triangles. Write the total number inside each triangle.

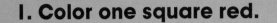

© Carson-Dellosa

Draw a line to match each number word to the correct numeral.

one	4
two	2
three	5
four	1
five	3

six	7
seven	10
eight	9
nine	6
ten	8

Connect the dots from 0 to 50. Start at the ★. Color the picture.

CD-104353

© Carson-Dellosa

Write the missing numbers.

1	2	3				7			10
11				15		17			
		24					28	29	
	32	33			36				
					46	47	48		
51			54						60
	63		65					69	70
71	72				76	77			
	82		84	85					
		93				97	98		100

Write the missing numbers.

A. _____, 47, 48

B. _____, 61, 62

C. _____, 13, 14

D. _____, 88, 89

E. _____, 94, 95

F. _____, 36, 37

G. 66, _____, 68

H. 81, _____, 83

I. 44, _____, 46

J. 79, _____, 81

K. 25, _____, 27

L. 98, _____, 100

M. _____, 7, _____

N. _____, 21, _____

O. _____, 34, _____

P. _____, 59, _____

Q. _____, 63, _____

R. _____, 72, _____

CD-104353

© Carson-Dellosa

Find the pattern in each row. Write the missing numbers.

A. 3, 4, _____, _____, 7, _____, _____

B. 5, 10, 15, _____, _____, 30, _____, 40

C. 4, 6, 8, _____, _____, 14, _____, 18

D. 46, 47, _____, 49, _____, _____, 52

E. 1, 3, 5, _____, _____, 11, 13, _____

F. 10, 20, _____, 40, _____, _____, 70

G. 3, 6, 9, _____, _____, 18, 21, _____

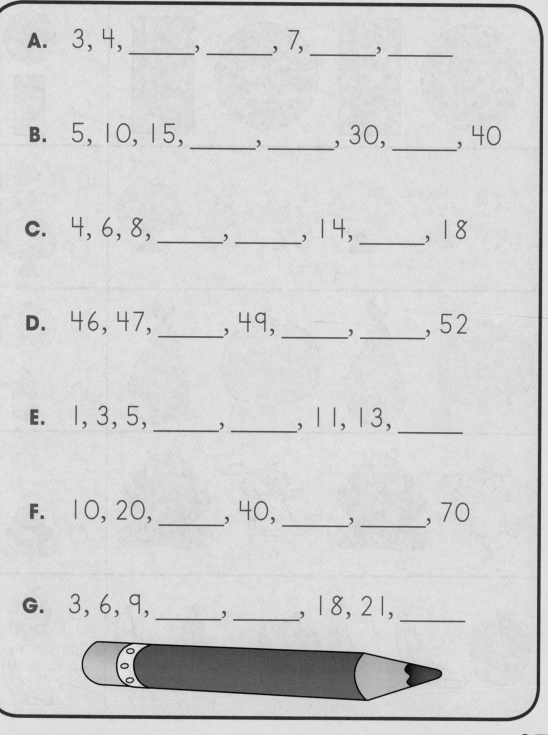

© Carson-Dellosa

Look at the pattern in each row. Fill in the circle beside the object that comes next.

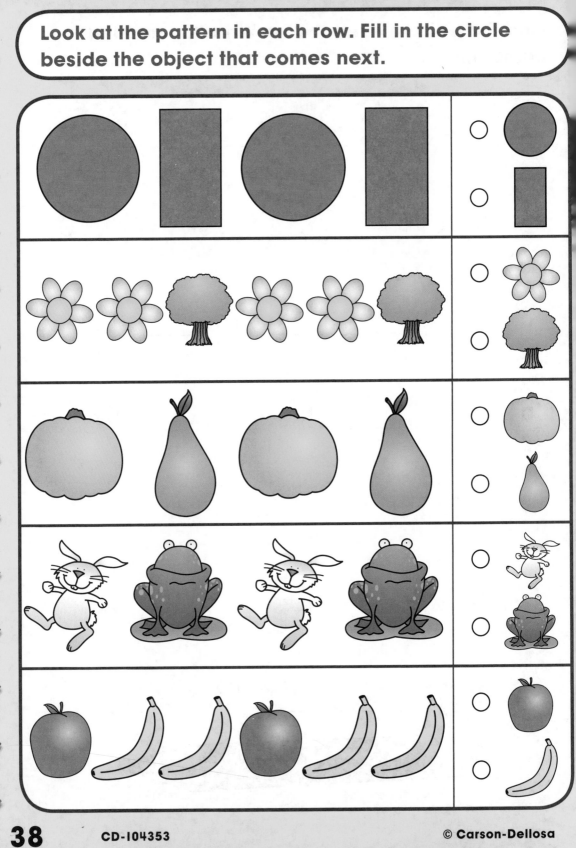

CD-104353 © Carson-Dellosa

Draw a line from each fish to the word that tells its place in line. Then, follow the directions.

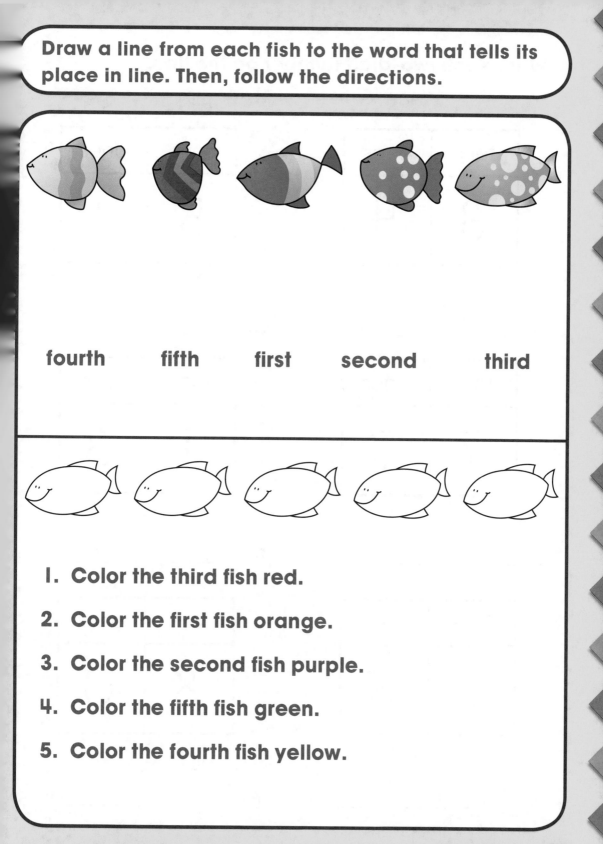

fourth   fifth   first   second   third

1. Color the third fish red.

2. Color the first fish orange.

3. Color the second fish purple.

4. Color the fifth fish green.

5. Color the fourth fish yellow.

Write each two-digit number on the line.

tens	ones
3	4

A. _____

tens	ones
5	1

B. _____

tens	ones
7	7

C. _____

tens	ones
1	3

D. _____

tens	ones
6	8

E. _____

tens	ones
8	0

F. _____

© Carson-Dellosa

Write > or < to compare each pair of numbers.

A. 10 ◯ 11   B. 44 ◯ 43

C. 34 ◯ 51   D. 59 ◯ 61

E. 63 ◯ 41   F. 72 ◯ 70

G. 19 ◯ 21   H. 86 ◯ 76

I. 27 ◯ 25   J. 91 ◯ 78

K. 49 ◯ 52   L. 33 ◯ 28

M. 17 ◯ 11   N. 89 ◯ 98

O. 72 ◯ 80   P. 46 ◯ 38

© Carson-Dellosa

Solve each problem. Use the pictures to help you.

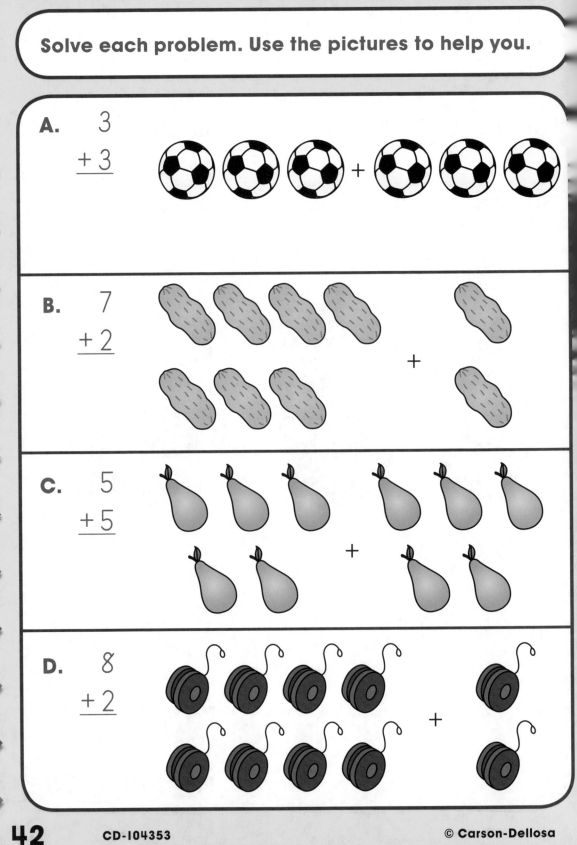

A.   3
      + 3

B.   7
      + 2

C.   5
      + 5

D.   8
      + 2

Solve each problem. Color the suns that have a sum of 9. How many suns did you color? _____

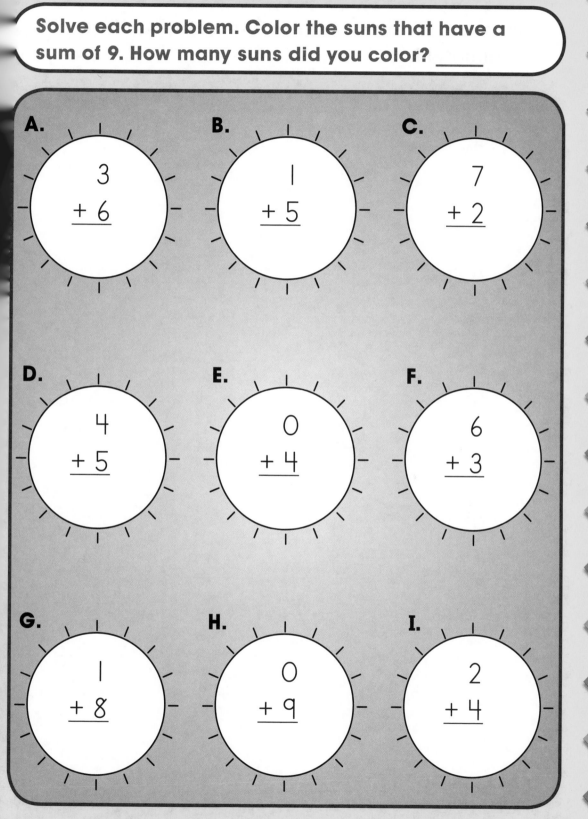

A.
$$\begin{array}{r} 3 \\ + 6 \\ \hline \end{array}$$

B.
$$\begin{array}{r} 1 \\ + 5 \\ \hline \end{array}$$

C.
$$\begin{array}{r} 7 \\ + 2 \\ \hline \end{array}$$

D.
$$\begin{array}{r} 4 \\ + 5 \\ \hline \end{array}$$

E.
$$\begin{array}{r} 0 \\ + 4 \\ \hline \end{array}$$

F.
$$\begin{array}{r} 6 \\ + 3 \\ \hline \end{array}$$

G.
$$\begin{array}{r} 1 \\ + 8 \\ \hline \end{array}$$

H.
$$\begin{array}{r} 0 \\ + 9 \\ \hline \end{array}$$

I.
$$\begin{array}{r} 2 \\ + 4 \\ \hline \end{array}$$

© Carson-Dellosa

How many problems can you solve correctly in two minutes?

A.
$$\begin{array}{r} 3 \\ +4 \\ \hline \end{array}\qquad \begin{array}{r} 7 \\ +1 \\ \hline \end{array}\qquad \begin{array}{r} 2 \\ +2 \\ \hline \end{array}\qquad \begin{array}{r} 3 \\ +3 \\ \hline \end{array}$$

B.
$$\begin{array}{r} 7 \\ +2 \\ \hline \end{array}\qquad \begin{array}{r} 4 \\ +2 \\ \hline \end{array}\qquad \begin{array}{r} 4 \\ +6 \\ \hline \end{array}\qquad \begin{array}{r} 6 \\ +0 \\ \hline \end{array}$$

C.
$$\begin{array}{r} 6 \\ +1 \\ \hline \end{array}\qquad \begin{array}{r} 3 \\ +6 \\ \hline \end{array}\qquad \begin{array}{r} 1 \\ +5 \\ \hline \end{array}\qquad \begin{array}{r} 5 \\ +5 \\ \hline \end{array}$$

D.
$$\begin{array}{r} 9 \\ +1 \\ \hline \end{array}\qquad \begin{array}{r} 10 \\ +0 \\ \hline \end{array}\qquad \begin{array}{r} 6 \\ +2 \\ \hline \end{array}\qquad \begin{array}{r} 2 \\ +3 \\ \hline \end{array}$$

E.
$$\begin{array}{r} 3 \\ +2 \\ \hline \end{array}\qquad \begin{array}{r} 3 \\ +5 \\ \hline \end{array}\qquad \begin{array}{r} 2 \\ +1 \\ \hline \end{array}\qquad \begin{array}{r} 5 \\ +2 \\ \hline \end{array}$$

Answers Correct: _____

CD-104353   © Carson-Dellosa

Solve each problem. Use the pictures to help you.

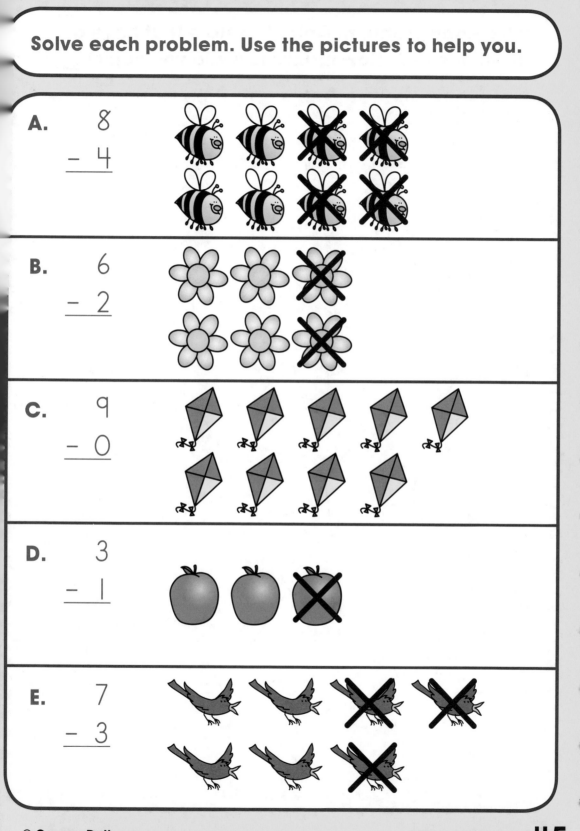

A. $\begin{array}{r} 8 \\ -\ 4 \\ \hline \end{array}$

B. $\begin{array}{r} 6 \\ -\ 2 \\ \hline \end{array}$

C. $\begin{array}{r} 9 \\ -\ 0 \\ \hline \end{array}$

D. $\begin{array}{r} 3 \\ -\ 1 \\ \hline \end{array}$

E. $\begin{array}{r} 7 \\ -\ 3 \\ \hline \end{array}$

© Carson-Dellosa

Solve each problem. Color the stars that have a difference of 3. How many stars did you color? _____

A.
8
− 5

B.
6
− 3

C.
4
− 2

D.
3
− 0

E.
7
− 5

F.
2
− 1

G.
9
− 6

H.
5
− 2

I.
4
− 1

CD-104353   © Carson-Dellosa

Solve each problem. Use the key to color the picture.

| = red 2 = blue 3 = yellow 4 = brown

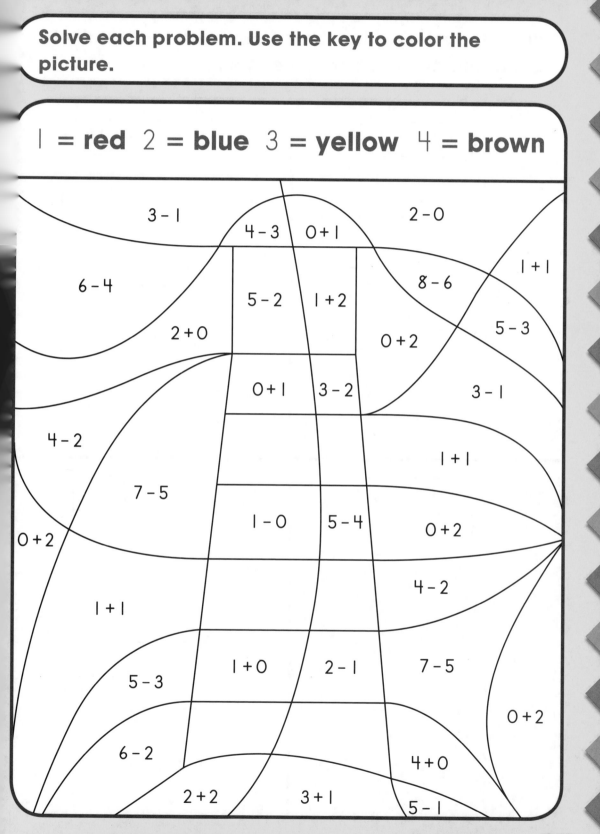

3 - 1
4 - 3   0 + 1
2 - 0
| + |
6 - 4
8 - 6
5 - 2 | + 2
5 - 3
2 + 0
0 + 2
0 + 1   3 - 2
3 - 1
4 - 2
| + |
7 - 5
| - 0   5 - 4   0 + 2
4 - 2
0 + 2
| + |
| + 0   2 - 1   7 - 5
5 - 3
0 + 2
6 - 2
4 + 0
2 + 2   3 + 1   5 - 1

© Carson-Dellosa

CD-104353   **47**

Write the missing numbers from each fact family to complete the number sentences.

A. $\boxed{2, 3, 5}$

$2 + 3 = \underline{\hspace{2cm}}$

$3 + \underline{\hspace{2cm}} = 5$

$5 - \underline{\hspace{2cm}} = 2$

$5 - 2 = \underline{\hspace{2cm}}$

B. $\boxed{4, 6, 10}$

$6 + \underline{\hspace{2cm}} = 10$

$4 + \underline{\hspace{2cm}} = 10$

$10 - 6 = \underline{\hspace{2cm}}$

$\underline{\hspace{2cm}} - 4 = 6$

C. $\boxed{3, 4, 7}$

$\underline{\hspace{2cm}} + 3 = 7$

$3 + 4 = \underline{\hspace{2cm}}$

$7 - \underline{\hspace{2cm}} = 4$

$7 - \underline{\hspace{2cm}} = 3$

D. $\boxed{1, 2, 3}$

$2 + 1 = \underline{\hspace{2cm}}$

$\underline{\hspace{2cm}} + 2 = 3$

$\underline{\hspace{2cm}} - 1 = 2$

$3 - 2 = \underline{\hspace{2cm}}$

CD-104353

© Carson-Dellosa

Solve each problem.

A.
```
  2
  3
+ 0
```

B.
```
  5
  1
+ 3
```

C.
```
  6
  2
+ 1
```

D.
```
  4
  0
+ 2
```

E.
```
  0
  6
+ 1
```

F.
```
  4
  3
+ 3
```

G.
```
  5
  1
+ 2
```

H.
```
  3
  3
+ 3
```

I.
```
  2
  2
+ 2
```

J.
```
  8
  1
+ 1
```

K.
```
  2
  5
+ 0
```

L.
```
  0
  4
+ 6
```

© Carson-Dellosa

Gavin had 8 crackers. Juliet had 3 crackers. Carla had 4 crackers.

1. Who had the most crackers?_____

2. Who had the fewest crackers?_____

3. How many crackers did they have

   in all?_____

Brandy cleaned her room. She found 3 sweaters and 6 shirts. She also found 2 socks and 8 shoes.

1. How many sweaters did Brandy find?_____

2. How many sweaters and shirts did Brandy find

   in all?_____

3. How many shoes and socks did Brandy find

   in all?_____

4. How many things did Brandy find in all? _____

Solve each problem.

A. $\begin{array}{r} 30 \\ + 10 \\ \hline \end{array}$

B. $\begin{array}{r} 90 \\ + 4 \\ \hline \end{array}$

C. $\begin{array}{r} 50 \\ + 40 \\ \hline \end{array}$

D. $\begin{array}{r} 34 \\ + 25 \\ \hline \end{array}$

E. $\begin{array}{r} 51 \\ + 42 \\ \hline \end{array}$

F. $\begin{array}{r} 77 \\ + 22 \\ \hline \end{array}$

G. $\begin{array}{r} 62 \\ + 16 \\ \hline \end{array}$

H. $\begin{array}{r} 46 \\ + 21 \\ \hline \end{array}$

I. $\begin{array}{r} 85 \\ + 11 \\ \hline \end{array}$

J. $\begin{array}{r} 33 \\ + 33 \\ \hline \end{array}$

K. $\begin{array}{r} 14 \\ + 13 \\ \hline \end{array}$

L. $\begin{array}{r} 28 \\ + 20 \\ \hline \end{array}$

Solve each problem.

A.
$$\begin{array}{r} 90 \\ -\ 30 \\ \hline \end{array}$$

B.
$$\begin{array}{r} 76 \\ -\ 20 \\ \hline \end{array}$$

C.
$$\begin{array}{r} 83 \\ -\ 80 \\ \hline \end{array}$$

D.
$$\begin{array}{r} 59 \\ -\ 40 \\ \hline \end{array}$$

E.
$$\begin{array}{r} 29 \\ -\ 19 \\ \hline \end{array}$$

F.
$$\begin{array}{r} 60 \\ -\ 10 \\ \hline \end{array}$$

G.
$$\begin{array}{r} 47 \\ -\ 31 \\ \hline \end{array}$$

H.
$$\begin{array}{r} 15 \\ -\ 13 \\ \hline \end{array}$$

I.
$$\begin{array}{r} 75 \\ -\ 22 \\ \hline \end{array}$$

J.
$$\begin{array}{r} 98 \\ -\ 51 \\ \hline \end{array}$$

K.
$$\begin{array}{r} 36 \\ -\ 23 \\ \hline \end{array}$$

L.
$$\begin{array}{r} 54 \\ -\ 44 \\ \hline \end{array}$$

CD-104353

© Carson-Dellosa

Draw lines to match the clocks that show the same time.

Write the time shown on each clock. The first one has been done for you.

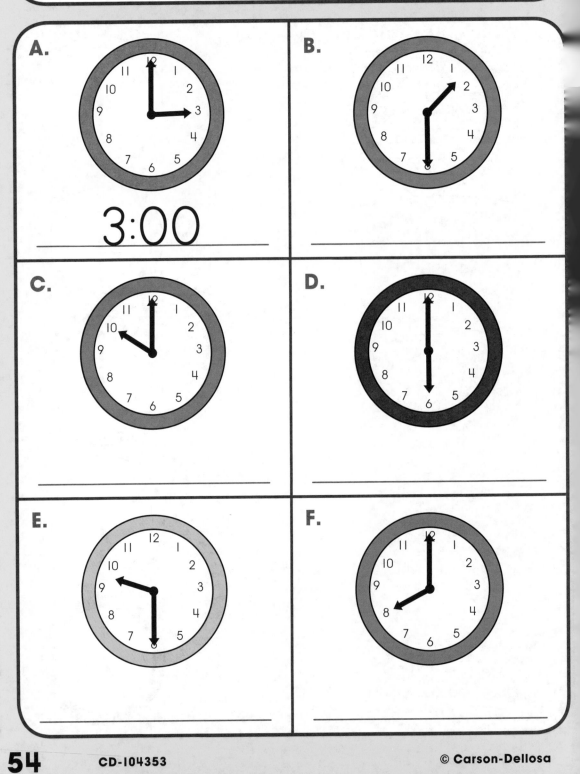

A.

3:00

B.

_____

C.

_____

D.

_____

E.

_____

F.

_____

© Carson-Dellosa

Write the missing dates on the calendar. Answer the questions.

October						
Sun.	Mon.	Tues.	Wed.	Thurs.	Fri.	Sat.
	1					
						13
		31				

1. **On what day of the week does October end?**

_____

_____

2. **How many Mondays are in October?**

_____

_____

3. **What day of the week is October 23?**

_____

_____

Each student in the class has one pet. Use the graph to answer the questions.

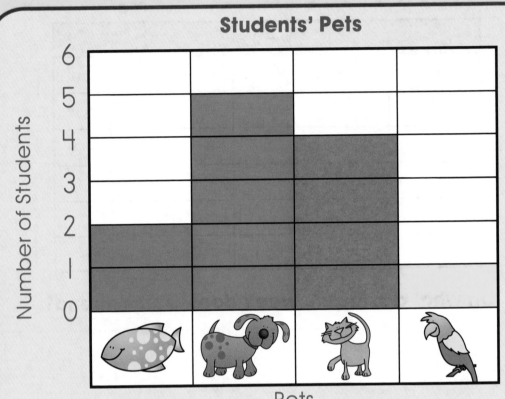

1. How many students have cats? _____

2. How many students have fish? _____

3. How many students have dogs? _____

4. How many students have birds? _____

5. How many students in all have pets? _____

CD-104353 © Carson-Dellosa

Use the table to complete the bar graph.

pears	IIII
apples	III
bananas	II
grapes	~~IIII~~ I

Students' Favorite Fruits

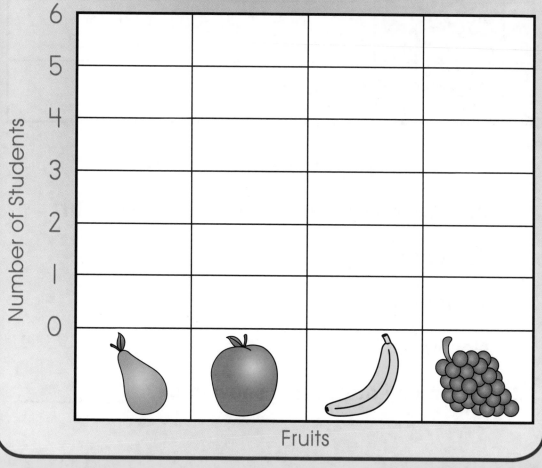

Number of Students

Fruits

© Carson-Dellosa

CD-104353

57

Use the graph to answer the questions.

Snowy Days

Months	Number of Snowy Days
November	❄
December	❄ ❄ ❄ ❄ ❄ ❄
January	❄ ❄ ❄ ❄ ❄ ❄ ❄
February	❄ ❄ ❄ ❄ ❄ ❄
March	❄ ❄

❄ = 1 snowy day

1. How many days did it snow in each month?

   January: _____

   February: _____

   November: _____

2. How many days did it snow in all? _____

CD-104353

© Carson-Dellosa

Circle the shapes that are divided in half.

Follow the directions.

A.

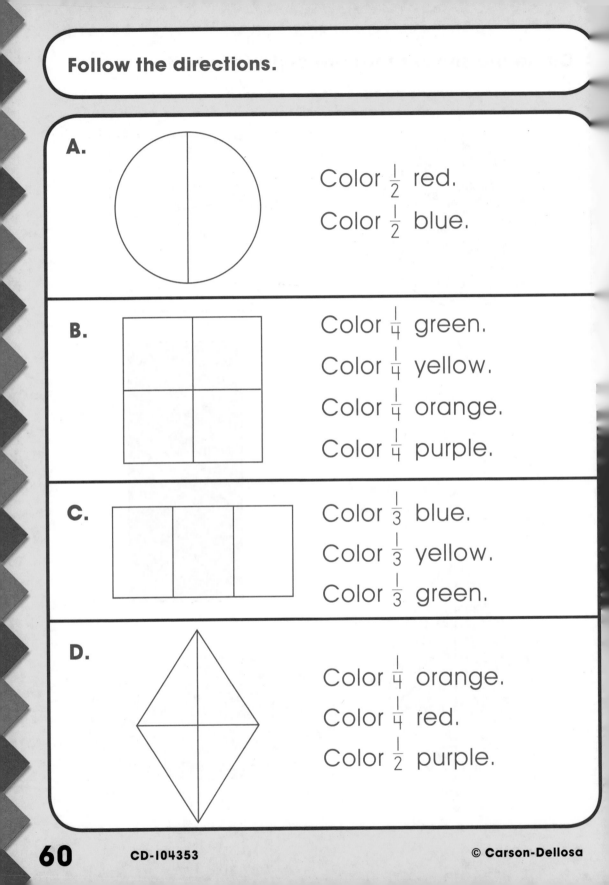

Color $\frac{1}{2}$ red.

Color $\frac{1}{2}$ blue.

B.

Color $\frac{1}{4}$ green.

Color $\frac{1}{4}$ yellow.

Color $\frac{1}{4}$ orange.

Color $\frac{1}{4}$ purple.

C.

Color $\frac{1}{3}$ blue.

Color $\frac{1}{3}$ yellow.

Color $\frac{1}{3}$ green.

D.

Color $\frac{1}{4}$ orange.

Color $\frac{1}{4}$ red.

Color $\frac{1}{2}$ purple.

CD-104353

© Carson-Dellosa